I0142480

GEORGE E. ROBINSON

LORD, WHY THE VALLEY?

LORD,
WHY THE VALLEY?

GEORGE E. ROBINSON

LORD, WHY THE VALLEY?

ISBN 978-1-7358211-5-3
George E. Robinson

Scripture quotations are from various versions of the Holy Bible.

For additional information, please contact:
lordwhythevalley@gmail.com.

For information about special discounts for bulk purchases please contact the Special Sales Department
Library of Congress Cataloging-in Publication Data

Published by Executive Business Writing
P.O. Box 10002, Moreno Valley, CA 92552
(951)268-0368
https://www.beverlycrockett.com
executivebusinesswriting@gmail.com

Edited by Julie Boney
JB Editing Solutions
www.jb-editingsolutions.com

Graphics designed by Tracy Spencer
Legacy Media, LLC
Moreno Valley, CA 92552

TABLE OF CONTENTS

FOREWORD

I was delighted when I was asked to read this anointed work written by my dear friend and now husband of six years, George E. Robinson. He is a compassionate, God-fearing man, who is no stranger to the highs and lows of life. His spiritual walk with God has provided him the fortitude to expand on such real, practical, and relevant information.

Lord, Why the Valley ? addresses the reality of life's ups and downs and ins and outs, and shines a light on the fact that there is a Redeemer who lives and will see you through the valley and walk you out to victory on the other side.

Carla Y. Robinson

Wife, Mother, Nana, Entrepreneur, and Realtor

INTRODUCTION

Valley – any depression lying between two high points of land

Perhaps you have been in a situation you didn't understand. Have you ever wondered aloud or in silence why you're in this place of despair? You say, I pay my tithes, I go to church, I even make more than one service from time to time. But I'm yet facing a dark cloud over my life. I hear the choir, and I understand the preacher's point, but after the last song and the benediction is done, I'm still faced with the lingering question, "Lord, why do I feel like I'm in this big, lonely valley?"

A valley is a depression lying between two high points of land. Our problems are like valleys – one low moment between two highs. I pray this book will awaken your inner strength and enlighten and encourage you to make it through your valley. Well, I pray this book will walk you out of that valley and into His presence.

Chapter 1

PROBLEMS OF LIFE

"*The Lord is my Shepherd; I shall not want*" (Psalm 23:1).

The problems of life are nothing new. As we all know, they don't discriminate. No one is omitted from life's challenges. There is elderly neglect, child abuse, racial profiling, gentrification, and mass shootings in schools and churches. These issues are compounded with homelessness, broken families, and global pandemics. These are among the many issues that have proven to be overwhelming, to say the least. As the saying goes, you cover your head and your feet are exposed, or you cover your feet and your head is exposed. Trouble is everywhere and constant. Whoever you are, from the pope to the pauper, you can't escape it. 1 Peter 4:12, 13 tells us, *"Beloved think it not strange concerning the fiery trial which is to try you, as though some strange thing happened unto you. But rejoice, inasmuch as ye are partakers of Christ's sufferings; that, when His glory is revealed, ye may be glad also with exceeding joy."* I don't have to convince you of trouble finding you no matter how many times you change your address. However, I can tell you there is a peace you can have in the midst of your valley experience. Philippians 4:7: *"And the peace of God, which passeth all understanding shall keep your hearts and minds in Christ Jesus."* In order to have this peace, you must FIRST know how to accept the Peacemaker.

Psalm 23:1: *"The Lord is my Shepherd; I shall not want."* David reached a point in his life in which the Lord was his source of ultimate peace, but David faced a valley of situations. David was the youngest of eleven sons of Jesse. As the story goes, Jesse didn't even think enough of David to present him to Samuel. But what God has for you that's right – it's for you. David was ultimately anointed in the presence of his father and ten brothers. Although God chose David, the relationship wasn't consummated until David was of age to enter union with God. That day finally came in the valley of Elah. It was at this time that the Philistines were at war with the children of Israel and a battle was imminent. The Philistines had the giant champion, Goliath, who belittled and taunted Israel with overwhelming size and power. By this time, however, David had gone through basic training as a shepherd. As a shepherd, David had successfully defended the sheep by slaying a lion and a bear. We must realize God would never put more on us than we're able to bear. Just as God was preparing David for greater things, God is preparing us as well.

David had reached that level of maturity and knew it. Therefore, when Goliath met David in that valley, mocked him, and disrespected God, something stood up in David, and that something was the Spirit of the living God. 1 Samuel 17:45, 46: "*Then said David to the Philistine, 'Thou comest to me with a sword, and with a spear, and with a shield: but I come to thee in the name of the Lord of hosts, the God of the armies of Israel, whom thou hast defied. This day will the Lord deliver thee into mine hand; and I will smite thee, and take thine head from thee, and I will give the carcasses of the host of the Philistines this day unto the fowls of the air, and to the wild beasts of the earth; that all the earth may know there is a God in Israel.*'"

These verses show us that David entered that valley knowing who God was. When we're facing a valley, we must believe Him to be the Shepherd of our soul. Do you know your Redeemer lives? Are you committed to the Lord, even when you're not perched on top of the mountain? We must hold fast to God even in the slowest of times. Romans 8:35: "*Who shall separate us from the love of Christ? shall tribulation, or distress, or persecution, or famine, or nakedness, or peril, or sword?*

Reaching a mature state in God is vital. When we reach that level in God, we stop falling for Satan's childish games. 1 Corinthians 13:11: "*When I was a child, I spake as a child, I understood as a child, I thought as a child: but when I became a man, I put away childish things.*" A child tends to lack, but an adult in Christ doesn't lack because the person realizes that God HAS and IS all that is needed. Although we're faced with many things, in whatsoever states, learn to be content. When we keep our eyes on the Lord, we can't sink (remember the story of Peter walking on the water).

"*I shall not want*" because God will supply our every need and it's according to His riches in glory. Did David misspeak? Were his words misquoted when he said, "*I shall not want*?" No, David realized that nothing could be better than God. You see you could gain the whole world and lose your soul.

Chapter 2

GREEN PASTURES

"*He makes me to lie down in green pastures*" (Psalm 23:2).

Despite your issues, trials, and tribulations, you were made to reign in healthier places. God didn't make us to fail; God has great plans for us. Jeremiah 29:11: *"'For I know the thoughts that I think toward you,' saith the Lord, 'thoughts of peace and not of evil, to give you an expected end.'"* God doesn't make mistakes or accidents; never give others the power to classify you as such, either. God made us in His image and likeness. Genesis 1:26: "*And God said, Let us make man in our image, after our likeness: and let them have dominion over the fish of the sea, and over the fowl of the air, and over the cattle, and over all the earth, and over all creeping thing that creepeth upon the earth.*" Yes, we were made to have dominance over creeps.

Now, before you take this and run, remember, we're no longer our own, but we've been bought with a price. 1 Corinthians 6:20: *"For ye are bought with a price: therefore, glorify God in your body, and in your spirit, which are God's."* A price was paid, which means control belongs to the Owner. We must submit our whole mind to

God, for this is our reasonable service according to Romans 12:1: *"I beseech ye therefore brethren, by the mercies of God, that ye present your bodies, a living sacrifice, holy, acceptable, unto God, which is your reasonable service."* God is calling for sheep, not goats. Goats butt against God while sheep look to the Shepherd for their protection and source of means.

We must realize that God's intention for us is to live in His kingdom (pastures). God's pasture isn't defined by natural location. You don't have to live in a mansion to feel His presence. You don't have to have thousands of dollars in the bank to be in His presence. You don't have to be an athlete, singer, movie star, or businessman to be in His presence. You just need to submit/surrender to God. Take the first step to His presence.

The prodigal son, after coming to himself, made his way home, and along the way he saw his father standing out looking and longing for his return. The father killed the fatted calf, put the ring on his son's hand, and welcomed him back into his presence. The Lord is waiting on you; just let go of what's keeping you from coming home.

Chapter 3

HE LEADS

"*He leadeth me beside still waters*" (Psalm 23:2).

In order to reach a destination, one must know where it is and how to get there. Everyone desires to be in a peaceful place, a place free of worry, strife, and trouble. Many have looked high and low, only to be met with disappointment. People are looking for this peace in all the wrong places – in sex, drugs, gangs, fame, or fortune. Although I can't speak from experience on each of the aforementioned, I can definitely speak on the peace of knowing Jesus as Lord and Savior. In His presence IS fullness of joy. Yielding to God has taken me from a state of worry into a peace that passeth all understanding. Philippians 4:7: *"And the peace of God which passeth all understanding, shall keep your hearts and minds through Christ Jesus."*

Jesus is the way, truth, and the life. Jesus is the only One who is qualified to lead us because He knows the way. The ways of a transgressor are hard. Proverbs 13:15: *"Good understanding giveth favor; but the way of transgressors is hard."*

Following Jesus requires us to read our road map, the Bible. It lets us know which way to go, which corners to turn. It tells us of impending pitfalls. Following Jesus will always lead us to the still waters of the Promised Land.

"*Still waters*" represents tranquility. Foolish people will never comprehend how to have it. The still waters can be obtained only by following the path that God has already laid. In order to hear God's voice while in the valley, we must close our eyes and open our hearts to God. When you seek God with your whole heart and not your eyes, He will fill you with such joy that your mouth will be forced to confess it.

The true believer will tell you, if you believe you will receive. Romans 10:20: *"For with the heart man believeth unto righteousness; and with the mouth confession is made unto salvation."* Faith comes by hearing; hearing, by the word of God. Who wouldn't want this peace from God? It's the fool that says there is no God. Let go and let God be captain of His ship.

Chapter 4

HE RESTORES

"*He restoreth my soul*" (Psalm 23:3).

Nobody ever said the valley would be easy. My yoke is easy, and my burden is light. We will experience burdens in life; however, God will not put more on us than we can bear. In this life there will be trying times that will try your peace, your joy, your patience, and your soul, but God will see you through every trying test, and in the midst of it all, He will restore to you what the locusts hath eaten. Joel 2:25: *"And I will restore to you the years the locust hath eaten, the cankerworm, the caterpillar, and the palmerworm, my great army which I sent among you."* Saved or not, everyone is open to attacks that wear on an individual, but the believer has a power Source that can never run low or run out. That Source is Jesus. I challenge you to call Him right now and see won't He answer. (Go ahead; I'll wait.)

Be not weary or give up in the valley because it says in Galatians 6:9, *"And let us not weary in well doing: for in due season, we will reap if we faint not."* To restore is to get something back to its original, intended state. Every believer needs time to get restored. If you neglect the signs, it will tell on anyone. Jesus was tempted of the devil after a forty-day fast, but afterward, Matthew 4:11 says, *"Then the devil leaveth Him, and behold, angels came and ministered unto Him."*

Even a glass of untouched water over a period of time will need to be restored due to the evaporation process. If the stationary glass must be restored, what about us? When Popeye would find himself on the wrong end of Bluto's fist, he would restore his super strength by reaching for his spinach. We have tools at our defense – His word, prayer, worship, and praise.

God's supply is limitless, so don't ever stop praising Him. Don't ever stop worshiping Him. Isaiah 40:31: *"But they that wait upon the Lord shall renew their strength; they shall mount with wings as eagles; they shall run, and not be weary; and they shall walk, and not faint."*

Chapter 5

CONTINUING THE JOURNEY

"*He leadeth me in the paths of righteousness for His name's sake*" (Psalm 23:3).

After God makes you, leads you, and restores you, it's time to continue the journey. You must realize victory isn't accomplished overnight. Ecclesiastes 9:11: "*I returned and saw under the sun, that the race is not to the swift, nor the battle to the strong....*"

We must yield to the leading of the Holy Spirit. Yes, Lord. I will go where you want me to go, I'll do what you want me to do, and I will say what you want me to say. God will never lead you astray. As sure as there is a way into the valley, there IS a way out. We walk by faith and not by sight. What the natural eye can't see your faith can. Your sight may say we're lost; your faith says He's making a way out of no way.

Numbers 23:19: "*God is a God that cannot lie neither the Son of man that He should repent.*" 1 Samuel 15:29: "*And also the Strength of Israel will not lie or repent; for He is not a man that He should repent.*"

When in your valley experiences, you must realize three things:

- You WILL go through something. 1 Peter 4:12: *"Beloved, think it not strange concerning the fiery trial which is to try you, as though some strange thing happened unto you."*
- You're never alone. Hebrews 13:5: "*...For he hath said, I will never leave thee, nor forsake thee.*"
- There is an expiration date. Psalm 30:5: "*Weeping may endure for a night, but joy cometh in the morning.*"

When you have been chosen by God, you will be considered a threat and therefore a target of the enemy. In the face of Satan's constant attacks, you must be consistent in the things of God. Don't forget your vow. Don't forget the love shown on the cross. Don't forget the reward for God's child and God's rebellious children. Sometimes, we must grin and bear it, but know this in the midst of it all: God is with us, and He IS for us.

Chapter 6

CONDITIONING FOR ATTACKS

"*Yea, though I walk through the valley of the shadow of death, I will fear no evil*" (Psalm 23:4).

Yea = although/may be but/so what/nevertheless.

We must condition ourselves in God to the point that Satan's traps and threats won't stop our determination to stay the course God has laid for us. Psalm 37:2: "*Fret not thyself because of evil doers.*"

When one realizes attacks are a part of life, it's then we are able to shift our focus from the problem to the solution. When problems present themselves, we get paralyzed by them. As we grow, we must realize that keeping our mind stayed on the solution rather than the problem will keep us in perfect peace (see Isaiah 26:3).

While in your valley, it's important to know that you're not alone, but that God is with you. While in the valley, one of your biggest battles is FEAR itself. Fear breeds doubt, which is the opposite of faith. You walk by faith, so when fear controls you, it stops you in your tracks. It prevents you from progressing. Fear has stopped many from even trying.

Some things in life are inevitable: death, taxes, and valleys. David realized he had to encounter a giant threat, but he had a "YEA" (Psalm 23:4). Goliath was bigger, stronger, more skilled, and more feared among the men, but David had heard enough of the enemies' taunting and took action (see 1 Samuel 17:40-50).

1 Samuel 17:48: *"And it came to pass, when the Philistine arose, and came and drew nigh to meet David, that David hasted, and ran toward the army to meet the Philistine."* David turned his walk in the valley of death to a sprint. When you're in the valley, your mind must already be convinced that you're on the winning side of the battle.

One key thing I want to convey to you, the reader, is this: Stop asking the wrong question in the valley. Don't ask God, "Why?" but ask, "What?" "Why" indicates a lack of God's choice, but "What" indicates your desire to understand the message behind it all. When troubles present themselves, we tend to ask God, "Why me? Why do I have to go through this? Why does he or she have it so easy? Why am I struggling?"

Why? Why? Why? I challenge you in your valley experience to change your WHY to a WHAT. Lord, what is it you want me to learn? What do you want me to do or say so I can teach others?

Job had to be corrected by God because he questioned his valley experience with the wrong questions (motives). God actually raised His own questions, which caused Job to humble himself. Job 42:5, 6: *"I have heard of thee by the hearing of the ear, but now mine eye seeth thee. Wherefore I abhor myself, and repent in dust and ashes."* Although we feel like victims when going through, we must never doubt God. He's still in control. The same God of the mountains IS the same God of the valley. Whether we run, sprint, jog, walk, or crawl, we must not stop moving through the valleys.

David walked through and not into the valley because he knew God was with him. When we are going through our valleys, sometimes we feel all alone, but we're not. God said He'd never leave us, nor forsake us. I know you're saying it sounds good to say that for this book, but it's true. In your relationship with God, who is holding whom? Philippians 3:12, *"...If that I may apprehend that for which also I am apprehended of Christ Jesus."*

In my own valley experience, I would feel overwhelmed and ready to give up and turn around, but God would always do something to keep me. My wife and I experienced financial hardship right before Covid hit. We were forced out of our townhome and had to stay with relatives. The valley was looking very dark, but in the midst of our trial I kept trusting and serving God. With no place to call our own and loss of employment, we were reduced to our trust and faith in God. Let me tell you, I found Him in my valley. Not only did God show up but showed out.

Today, with less, God has put us in a townhome costing more than the prior, and we have been able to purchase a new vehicle. We have an abundance of food in the refrigerator, gas in the car, and all the bills paid, with enough left to have money in our accounts. I found out in the valley that God has an accounting system that will baffle a CPA, but it works.

I also realize that God is always speaking. The question is, are we listening? Our trials have a way of drowning out the voice of the Lord. This is why we must develop a prayer life. Prayer brings us before the presence of God and in His presence is fullness of joy. In His presence is the perfect time to hear from God regarding an answer to your WHY question.

Chapter 7

HE COMFORTS

"*Thy rod and thy staff they comfort me*" (Psalm 23:4).

Stepping outside of our comfort zone can create a moment of uncertainty, but take that step in Jesus' name because your steps are ordered by the Lord. You're under assignment. God won't send you unequipped, but He will be with you even in the time of trouble. Like sheep, we sometimes stray and get trapped in the thickets of life, but God, the Shepherd of our soul, can use His long Shepherd's staff, which has a hook shape to it, to reach us and pull us out of the pit of trouble. Sometimes, we don't stray, but danger still will pursue us in the form of the wolf. That same staff God used to rescue us when we strayed can be used from the other, pointed, end to save us from our predator, Satan.

God never said the valley wasn't dangerous, but He never said it couldn't be conquered. We can do all things through Christ which strengthens us. Continue to trust in the Lord. Take your journey one step at a time, one foot in front of the other; don't look back because what you need is before you. What is behind you is your past, but the best is yet to come. Remind yourself, I've got to reach my destiny. I can reach that mountain top.

In your valley there will be people who count themselves as enemies. Enemies are those who oppose your goal; they try to stop or hinder you from reaching your goal. Your enemy may not even know you but may know what you're trying to do.

Sometimes you'll be opposed because of who you are, and sometimes because of who you represent. Don't take it personally but do take it seriously. I can't tell you how long you'll be in the valley, but I can tell you God has a seat reserved for you at His table. Yes, God can and will provide relief during your journey and His anointed can get a reservation to sit at His table, which means the enemy can't touch you while in His presence. In the midst of your valley, God has prepared a feast, so if you need joy, it's on the table; peace, it's on the table; love, it's on the table; whatever it is, it's on the table.

We must remember, the blessings in life that we receive from God's table are just to refresh us along our way. Some people confuse the blessings from His table as the actual goal. The actual goal is to be evermore in His presence. As the song goes, "I'd rather have Jesus than silver and gold," or my version, "I'd rather have Jesus AND silver and gold."

It's during our travel through the valley that God deposits His anointing upon us. If we don't go through something, we can't get to the other side. An anointing is something placed upon us, a gift from God. We must learn to use His anointing placed on our lives. We are anointed by God to overcome the enemy.

David was anointed to later lead his people. David wasn't his father, Jesse's, first, second, or third choice, but he was God's choice. Stop looking for man to validate your anointing. When God calls, He also qualifies. The anointing from God is more than enough to accomplish your task. When God anoints you, it runneth over, so don't hold back your anointing by not reaching out to others because you have needs. Remember Joseph. He was anointed to interpret dreams (see Genesis 40). Joseph's valley was a prison, but Joseph shows you that your gift (if you use it) will make room for you.

While in the valley, don't stop doing the things God instructed you to do and be. If God is the God of the mountain and the valley, then we must be His people, whether in the valley or on the mountain. Don't let your dejection determine your location in God. Anything worth having is worth fighting for, so fight the good fight of faith; lay hold of it.

Chapter 8

VALLEY OF THE BONES

"*Son of man, can these bones live*?" (Ezekiel 37:3).

Sometimes we find ourselves in valleys surrounded by graves full of dry bones, but know from Romans 8:28 that "*All things work together for the good of them that love the Lord and are called according to his purpose.*" It's in your valley that God proves to you, your grave, your enemies, and Satan that He is God and will perform it just like He said He would. Ezekiel 37:13-14: "*And ye shall know that I am the Lord, when I have opened your graves, O my people, and brought you up out of your graves. And shall put my spirit in you, and ye shall live, and I shall place you in your own land: then shall ye know that I, the Lord, have spoken it, and performed it, saith the Lord.*"

I thought I was finished with this book when the Lord asked me, "What about the readers who have already fallen victim to Satan's attacks?" It was then that the Lord reminded me of the valley of the bones. The Lord reminded me of what Solomon tells us: There's nothing new under the sun. This statement stands true regarding what Ezekiel saw because if you look around, you can see the same thing and for some of us you don't have to look far. I see many bones in the valley. Bones were designed to be frames which support the body.

God showed me that many people have lost the fight in their valley experience because they allowed the devil to strip them of their anointing, dreams, and focus. As sure as the devil is a destroyer, the Lord is a Restorer. No matter how long or how dry your situation may appear, you must come to realize God can do anything but fail. Sometimes it may seem there is no hope or chance, but God is saying, "Not so."

God asked Ezekiel and I'm asking you, the reader, can your dry situation be revived? You must acknowledge that God can restore you. The question wasn't asked because God wasn't sure; it was asked to get you to think and confess. Once this is done, God knows whether you're ready. In your valley, God will speak, so be slow to speak and quick to hear God's word.

As I began to reflect back, I saw what I couldn't see then. I had experienced a dark period in my life in which I wanted to give in while I was in my valley of financial woes. I all but said there was no hope, but guess what! After several sunrises and sunsets, I finally figured out what was wrong.

1. I had to walk by faith, not sight.
2. I had to give God a "yet" praise and worship.

3. I had to have the mind of a giver, not a taker.
4. I had to focus on the solution (Jesus), not the problem. You see I had to practice what I've said and heard preached over my lifetime. I had a saying I've quoted for years: "The problem ain't the problem; it's the way you see it; that's the problem."

Through my own valley I was able to hear God. He told me to write the vision and make it plain so the one fighting to make it out of the valley, and those who get stuck in it can build their faith to make it. You see, as you read through this book, I prophesy you're coming out! I prophesy that every scattered dry bone in your life is reassembled and restored. Failure is not an option in God; you shall live and not die. I want you to repeat this out loud, "I shall live through this valley experience and not die. I will, I must fulfill my destiny in Jesus' name, Amen."

Now, pause and meditate on what you just confessed. You see, once you confess with your mouth and believe it with your heart you are saved; saved from the shadow of the valley of death. You don't have to fear the evil for God is with you.

Ok, now that you were prophesied over, God showed me in Ezekiel 37:10 that after the prophecy is spoken over you, a word must be spoken over the situation. Therefore, I speak . . .

- Deliverance
- Healing
- Joy
- Peace
- Wholeness

In Jesus' name.

Chapter 9

LOOKING FORWARD

"Prophesy to these bones, and say to them, 'O dry bones, hear the word of the Lord'" (Ezekiel 37:4).

OK, you have come this far in your valley, so don't look back. What you long for is before you. I'm reminded of an email I received about a stranded climber. It went something like this: "A man was climbing a big mountain one day alone when suddenly the hook dislodged, causing the climber to free fall. After finally being stopped by the safety line, the climber began to pray as he hung helplessly, facing the sky. All of a sudden, the Lord spoke to the climber and said, 'I have heard your cry and have come to save you.' The climber said, 'OK, Lord, what must I do to be saved?' To his shock, the Lord said, 'Cut the rope.' The climber, doubting he heard God right, asked again, but the answer was the same, 'Cut the rope.' After several hours of deciding what to do, the climber decided not to cut the rope, and he eventually died on the rope, but what the climber didn't know was that he was a safe drop from land."

Grave Situation

In this valley God showed me graves – graves of people who for one reason or another got trapped and dried up in the valley. As I examined the graves I saw marriages in the graves, family graves, missionary graves, pastor graves, bone fragments from joy, peace, and love. As I looked about the many graves, the question was posed, can these dry bones in the valley live again? It was at this point that I went from being spectator to being in my very own coffin. It was here I found out what being in a "grave situation" felt like. It was then I began to fight; I found a strong will to live in spite of my situation.

Chapter 10

WAITING IN FAITH

"I see four men loose, … and the form of the fourth is like the Son of God" (Daniel 3:25).

I realize that faith is an action word. While we don't know our breaking point and/or how much we can take, God knows and won't put more on us than we can bear. I found as I lay in that grave that it isn't over until God says it's over. I took my eyes off the problem and put them on God. When you're lying in a grave you can't help but look up. As I came to myself like the prodigal in the hog pen, I began to pray out loud, and then my prayer turned into a praise. You see, even when you reach a roadblock in life, your praise can go where you physically can't. Remember, I waited patiently on the Lord, and He heard my cry (see Psalm 40).

It was at this point I began to see things in third person. As I first saw myself helplessly lying in a coffin I could also see above ground. I saw a valley full of coffins containing dry bones. Most were silent with the exception of a few, which carried faint noises. Suddenly, in the distance appeared an image like the Son of God (that same image the three Hebrews saw in the furnace). The image was tiptoeing throughout the valley. I began to wonder aloud at what I was seeing when the image said keep praising, because I'm looking for signs of life and your praises will lead me to you. Whatever you do, don't stop praising. It was at this moment I was back in the grave and began to praise God and beat upon the inside of that coffin with everything in me. As I prayed, praised, and pounded, I began to hear the sound of "chip, chip, chip..." As the sound got louder I asked aloud what it was. A voice as of the sound of many rivers said, "Be not dismayed for it is the Lord your God, and the sound you hear is the "SHOVEL of DELIVERANCE."

As excitement filled my once dry bones the sound stopped and was replaced by silence. After a moment of silence, I began to hear a jingling. No one had to tell me what this sound was for I remember reading Revelation 1:18, which said that God took the keys of death. Yes, the jingling was the keys that would unlock me from my grave situation. I don't care how deep the grave is or how long you have been there, God has the shovel and the key, but you must provide the faith and praise for Him to rescue you. Remember, God has no respect of persons. What He did for one, He'll do for another.

Chapter 11

GOODNESS AND MERCY

"*Surely goodness and mercy shall follow me all the days of my life, and I will dwell in the house of the Lord forever*" (Psalm 23:6).

As you reach the end of this book, I pray you've reached the beginning of a brand-new start. "Lord, why the valley?" should be replaced with "Lord, I'm ready. Show me what you want me to get from my valley experience."

There are several things you must remember:

- God is in the driver's seat for He leadeth us.
- Because you're in a valley doesn't mean you're being punished or deserving of some bad fate.
- Make sure you're asking the right questions to the right person.

When we go before God seeking direction and meaning it, then we understand our mission, and we understand that the process is more bearable.

Ministry means to serve. Some of the things we encounter are to us a greater witness for others trying to find their way. So, as you read this book maybe . . .

1. Your marriage is under attack.
2. Your children are giving you problems.

3. Your finances are low.
4. Your health is ailing.
5. Your search for work seems bleak.
6. You're facing foreclosure.
7. Your rent is due, and the baby needs formula.

Well, don't give up, I've already prayed for you.

INSPIRATIONAL QUOTES WITH SPACE FOR NOTES

1. "I Know Why the Caged Bird Sings" ~ Isaiah 53:5: *"But He [was] wounded for our transgressions, [He was] bruised for our iniquities: the chastisement of our peace [was] upon him; and with his stripes we are healed."* ~ God can free you (bird) from any and all your pain, your praise (song) is the key. Now shout hallelujah!

____

____

____

2. "Let's Be Reasonable" ~ Romans 12:1: *"...present your bodies a living sacrifice, holy, acceptable unto God, [which is] your reasonable service."* ~ In my Anita Baker voice "Giving You the Best That I Got." Question: Are you a giver? If, so how?

____

____

____

3. "Get Your Swagger Back" ~ Romans 4:20: *"He staggered not at the promise of God through unbelief; but*

was strong in faith, giving glory to God." ~ Put some pep back in your step. God cannot lie; He will do what He said He would do, so walk around your Jericho wall like you know it's coming down!
Don't trip, God's got this!

____

____

____

4. "Be Still" ~ Psalm 46:10: "*Be still, and know that I [am] God: I will be exalted among the heathen, I will be exalted in the earth.*" ~ Remember when your mother would tell you to stop moving your head while she was trying to comb it, Well God is trying to fix our head, but we need to "BE STILL, "so He can finish.
Thought I would share again ... be blessed and hold still!

____

____

____

5. "This One Is on the House" ~ John 7:37: "*In the last day, that great [day] of the feast, Jesus stood and cried, saying, If any man thirst, let him come unto Me, and* *drink."* ~ This drink doesn't leave you with a hangover. The price has already been paid and it will quench your longing. So, what are you waiting on?

___

___

___

6. "Change Is Coming" ~ Revelation 21:4: "*And God shall wipe away all tears from their eyes; and there shall be no more death, neither sorrow, nor crying, neither shall there be any more pain: for the former things are passed away.*" ~ If you just hold on, it will be worth the wait. I'm praying for you. You're gonna make it!

___

___

___

7. "Billie Jean Is Not My Lover" ~ Luke 16:13: "*No servant can serve two masters: for either he will hate the one, and love the other; or else he will hold to the one, and despise the other. Ye cannot serve God and mammon.*" ~ Nobody in their right mind wants a part time lover, and God is no different.

Giving Him (God), the best that I got (Anita Baker and Michael Jackson)

____

____

____

8. "Can I Get a Witness?" ~ 1 John 5:10: *"He that believeth on the Son of God hath the witness in himself: he that believeth not God hath made Him a liar..."* ~ Has God done anything for you? Well, if it's in you, let's hear it.

____

____

____

9. "Something Don't Feel Right" ~ Proverbs 16:25: *"There is a way that seemeth right unto a man, but the end thereof [are] the ways of death."* ~ But he/she looks so good. But it's easy money. But no one will know. I'll just do it this one time. You'd better listen to that something (God) telling you don't do it. A moment of compromise can lead to a lifetime of consequences.

____

____

____

10. "It's a Matter of Life and Death" ~ Proverbs 18:21: *"Death and life [are] in the power of the tongue: and they that love it shall eat the fruit thereof."* ~ Watch what you say. It can determine your fate. Going through, speak breakthrough. Battling sickness, speak healing. Struggling financially, speak prosperity. Facing a dead situation, speak life. Whatever it is, speak over your situation in Jesus' name, Amen!

____

____

____

11. "So, What's New?" ~ Lamentations 3:21-23: *"This I recall to my mind; therefore have I hope. [It is of] the LORD'S mercies that we are not consumed, because His compassions fail not. [They are] new every morning: great [is] Thy faithfulness."* ~ Well, God did it again; He woke us up this morning! How will you show your gratitude?

____

____

____

12. "To Be or Not to Be" ~ That is the question you must be prepared to answer. Be who God made you to be. Don't change for anyone but God. ~ 1 Peter 1:15, 16: "*But as He which hath called you is holy, so be ye holy in all manner of conversation. Because it is written, Be ye holy; for I am holy.*"
Mold me and shape me.

____

____

____

13. "Sleeping with the Enemy" ~ Judges 16:19: "*And she made him sleep upon her knees; and she called for a man, and she caused him to shave off the seven locks of his head; and she began to afflict him, and his strength went from him.*" ~ Be careful where you lay your head, and every knee wasn't meant to be.
Rest in the Lord.

____

____

____

14. "Hide 'n Seek" ~ Psalm 27:5: "*For in the time of trouble He shall hide me in His pavilion: in the secret of His tabernacle shall He hide me; He shall set me up upon a rock.*" ~ God will conceal you from the fiery threats of the enemy, but you have to seek His will concerning you.

____

____

____

15. "Dressed to Impress!" ~ Ephesians 6:11: "*Put on the whole armor of God, that ye may be able to stand against the wiles of the devil.*" ~ Did you forget something this morning? Not your keys, your wallet, your money, or your cell phone. I'm talking about your garment to fight the devil because he will try you.
Put on the garment of Praise!

____

____

____

16. "WWJD?" ~ John 19:30: "*When Jesus therefore had received the vinegar, He said, It is finished: and He bowed his head, and gave up the ghost.*" ~ He would finish the job even if it cost Him his life. No greater love. Follow your heavenly Father's example and finish what you started.

What Would Jesus Do?

____

____

____

17. "Got Milk?" ~ 1 Peter 2:2: "*As newborn babes, desire the sincere milk of the word, that ye may grow thereby.*" ~ (Milk = An extracted substance containing nourishment). What's in your glass? Don't leave your drink unattended at anyone's party.

Have a glass on the house!

____

____

____

18. "I Want to Give a Shout-Out to..." ~ Joshua 6:5: *"...[and] when ye hear the sound of the trumpet, all the people shall shout with a great shout; and the wall of the city shall fall down flat..."* ~ ...All those walls in my life. COME DOWN IN JESUS NAME!!!
Wow, now didn't that feel good!

____

____

____

19. "Don't Start None, Won't Be None" ~ Matthew 16:19: *"And I will give unto thee the keys of the kingdom of heaven: and whatsoever thou shalt bind on earth shall be bound in heaven: and whatsoever thou shalt loose on earth shall be loosed in heaven."* ~ The key to victory starts with you and ends with God. We start it God finishes it!

____

____

____

20. "Don't Believe the Hype" ~ Luke 8:52: *"And all wept, and bewailed her: but He said, Weep not; she is not*

dead, but sleepeth." ~ I know what the doctor said, the lawyer said, the haters said, family said, doubters said, and I know what you thought, but what did God say?
Whose report will you believe?

____

____

____

21. "In the Midst of It All" ~ Psalm 138:7: "*Though I walk in the midst of trouble, thou wilt revive me: thou shalt stretch forth thine hand against the wrath of mine enemies, and thy right hand shall save me.*" ~ Even in troubling times God is extending his hand of compassion to shield you from the attack. He may not stop trouble, but He'll see you through it!

____

____

____

22. "Let the Past Be the Past" ~ Philippians 3:13: "*Brethren, I count not myself to have apprehended: but [this] one thing [I do], forgetting those things which are behind, and reaching forth unto those things which are* *before...*" ~ We all have regrets in life, but you don't have to dwell on it. Let go and let God, for His grace is sufficient. Experience is speaking.

____

____

____

23. "It's All Good" ~ Genesis 50:20: "*But as for you, ye thought evil against me; [but] God meant it unto good, to bring to pass, as [it is] this day, to save much people alive.*" ~ Beware all haters, you thought it would kill me, but I'm using it as a steppingstone.
What don't kill you makes you stronger.

____

____

____

24. "A Yet Praise" ~ Habakkuk 3:18: "*Yet I will rejoice in the LORD, I will joy in the God of my salvation.*" ~ I ain't out of it yet, but I'm still gonna praise Him, because I will get out of it. I ain't through it yet, but I'm praising my way through it!
Praise is my weapon!

____

____

____

25. "Simon Says..." ~ Luke 5:5: "*And Simon answering said unto Him, Master, we have toiled all the night, and have taken nothing: nevertheless, at thy word I will let down the net.*" ~ Don't give up because you tried and didn't get the results you hoped for. If God tells you to let down your net then just trust Him. Delayed don't mean denied!

Be persistent.

____

____

____

26. "Blame It on the Alcohol" ~ Proverbs 20:1: "*Wine [is] a mocker, strong drink [is] raging: and whosoever is deceived thereby is not wise.*" ~ We see what it does when driving, we see what it does to marriages, we see what it does to decision making, we see what it does to finances, yet it still deceives. Just ask God to deliver you from deception. (You're not a bad person, just a person with a bad habit)

____

____

____

27. I Can't Take It!" ~ 1 John 3:5: "*And ye know that He was manifested to TAKE AWAY our sins; and in Him is no sin.*" ~ It's a God situation; you can't erase it, stop it, replace it, or ignore it, but God took care of it on the cross. We have an advocate who can do anything but fail. (Give it to Jesus and leave it.) Need a prayer partner? I'm just an in-box away and God is just a prayer away.

____

____

____

28. "Just Who Do You Think You Are?" ~ Acts 19:15: "*And the evil spirit answered and said, Jesus I know, and Paul I know; but who are ye?*" ~ Don't play with the devil, without God you don't stand a snowball's chance in hell of making it. (Remember it ain't about you, but the God that lives in you.)

29. "Don't Get It Twisted!" ~ Isaiah 5:20: "*Woe unto them that call evil good, and good evil...*" ~ Stop trying to make God what you want Him to be and be what He intended you to be. (Stop trying to rewrite what God said.)

30. "Stand for Something Or Fall for Anything" ~ Galatians 5:1" "*Stand fast therefore in the liberty wherewith Christ hath made us free and be not entangled again with the yoke of bondage.*" ~ Look, you been there, done that. Drop it like a bad habit and take a stand against the haters (that devil).

31. "Drop It Like It's Hot" ~ Colossians 2:21, 22: "(*Touch not; taste not; handle not; Which all are to perish with the using;*)..." ~ If the label on the package doesn't say God Approved, don't touch it. Beware of knock-off brands. They never stand up to the real thing. Just like fake jewelry, it'll turn colors on you.

____

____

____

32. "All You Had to Do Was Ask" ~ James 4:2: "*Ye lust, and have not: ye kill and desire to have, and cannot obtain: ye fight and war, yet ye have not, because ye ask not.*" ~ Stop wanting what other people have and get what God has for you. Just meet His requirements and ask. (PS. Some things you think you want, but you don't realize you don't need them. God's actually doing you a favor by not giving them to you.)

____

____

____

33. "Have You Checked Your Filter?" ~ Matthew 6:21: *"For where your treasure is, there will your heart be also."* ~ The mind is a filter to the heart. NOTHING can get into your heart unless it goes through the filter of your mind, good or bad (see Philippians 4:8-9).

____

____

____

34. "Never Say What You Will Or Will Not Do" ~ Romans 7:15: *"I do not understand what I do. For what I want to do I do not do, but what I hate I do."* ~ It's in man's DNA to do the things we say we would or wouldn't do. This is why we need a blood transfusion from God. Thank God for the blood of Jesus!

____

____

____

35. "Get Your Grant Here" ~ Ephesians 3:16: *"That He would grant you, according to the riches of His glory, to be strengthened with might by His Spirit in the inner man..."* ~ No matter what subject you're undertaking, this grant will apply. See God for details on how to redeem the grant.

____

____

____

36. "April Fool" ~ Psalm 53:1: "*The fool hath said in his heart, [There is] no God.*" ~ Don't be fooled. God is very real. How do you think you made it this far? Looks, money...

____

____

____

37. "Amazing Grace" ~ John 1:17: "*For the law was given by Moses, [but] grace and truth came by Jesus Christ.*" ~ Lord, thank you. If it weren't for your grace I dread to think where I would be. Like a ship without a sail! If you want to thank Him, testify to His grace!

____

____

____

38. "Transformers, More Than Meets the Eye" Romans 12:2: "*And be not conformed to this world: but be ye transformed by the renewing of your mind, that ye may prove what [is] that good, and acceptable, and perfect will of God.*" ~ We tend to spend more time on the outer appearance and neglect the inner. Outer beauty is fading, but inner beauty can last a lifetime.

____

____

____

39. "Dancing with Wolves" ~ Matthew 10:16: "*Behold, I send you forth as sheep in the midst of wolves: be ye therefore wise as serpents, and harmless as doves.*" ~ You can't beat Satan at his game, so change your approach by dancing to God's tune. I challenge you to get your praise on, even in the midst of your enemies!

____

____

____

40. "In God We Trust" ~ Psalm 118:8: *"[It is] better to trust in the LORD than to put confidence in man."* ~ If God says he's coming back for a prepared people, BELIEVE HIM.

____

____

____

41. "If You Don't Stand for Something, You'll Fall for Anything" ~ Exodus 14:13: *"And Moses said unto the people, Fear ye not, stand still, and see the salvation of the LORD, which He will shew to you today..."* ~ Stand on the promises of God and He will deliver. Don't give in to the fear of your situation. (Speaking from experience.)

____

____

____

42. "I Feel Something Coming over Me" ~ Deuteronomy 28:2: *"And all these blessings shall come on thee, and overtake thee, if thou shalt hearken unto the voice of the LORD thy God."* ~ Lord, I'm listening. Have your way. I need thee oh! How I need thee. Every hour all the day I need thee. Oh, bless me now my Saviour....

___

___

___

43. "You Won the Fight, but Did You Win the Battle?" Matthew 16:26: "*For what is a man profited, if he shall gain the whole world, and lose his own soul? or what shall a man give in exchange for his soul?*" ~ You may rejoice because you have a 6-figure income and live on sugar hill, but if you don't have Jesus, it don't mean a thing.

___

___

___

44. "Are You a Spectator Or Participator?" ~ James 1:23, 24: "*For if anyone is a hearer of the word and not a doer, he is like a man observing his natural face in a mirror; for he observes himself, goes away, and immediately forgets what kind of man he was.*" ~ And don't be a procrastinator or perpetrator. Life is too short.

---

45. "Just Passing Through" ~ Psalm 23:4: "*Yea, though I walk through the valley of the shadow of death, I will fear no evil: for thou [art] with me; thy rod and thy staff they comfort me.*" ~ Don't look at it as going through, but rather as passing through. Remember, life and death are in the power of the tongue.

---

46. "It's Not How You Start, but How You Finish That Counts" ~ Luke 13:30: "*And, behold, there are last which shall be first, and there are first which shall be last.*" ~ Not married yet? No job yet? No house yet? No peace yet? Well just remember, delayed ain't denied. Good things come to those who wait upon the Lord. Just receive this and say Amen!

47. "Don't Succumb but Overcome" ~ Romans 12:21: *"Be not overcome of evil, but overcome evil with good."* ~ Stop letting the devil push you around and push back. Stop reacting to things and start enacting things.

48. "It's All in the Approach" ~ Hebrews 4:16: *"Let us therefore come boldly unto the throne of grace, that we may obtain mercy, and find grace to help in time of need."* ~ What you need to do is take it to the Lord and when you finish leave it there.

49. "Keep the Faith" ~ 2 Timothy 4:7: *"I have fought a good fight, I have finished [my] course, I have kept the faith..."* ~ It's not always about winning and losing, but sometimes God just wants to know if we're committed to Him. Everything ain't going your way, so just keep the faith and know all things work together for our good.

____

____

____

50. "On Your Mark, Get Set, GO!" ~ Habakkuk 2:2: *"And the LORD answered me, and said, Write the vision, and make [it] plain upon tables, that he may RUN that readeth it."* ~ This may be good reading, but what good is reading it if you don't apply it? Faith without works is dead, so get GOING! and see the manifestation of God revealed.

____

____

____

51. "Don't Go There" ~ Genesis 26:2: *"And the LORD appeared unto him, and said, 'Go not down into*

Egypt; dwell in the land which I shall tell thee of.'" ~ Stay the course God has set for you and don't be distracted by the devil's evil influences. Remember, you're better than that. (Also read Genesis 26:3)

____

____

____

52. "Hold It; Don't Say Another Word" ~ Exodus 14:14: "*The LORD shall fight for you, and ye shall hold your peace.*" ~ God's got this one, so sit back and watch Him do what He does. You ain't gotta say a word.

____

____

____

53. "Right This Way, Please. Your Table Is Ready" ~ Psalm 23:5: "*Thou preparest a table before me in the presence of mine enemies...*" ~ What God has for you, it's for you, no matter who doesn't like it. You're God's guest. Will you accept His invitation? (I'm not just talking salvation, but it's on the table.)

54. "What You Don't Know Can Kill YOU" ~ John 5:39: *"Search the scriptures; for in them ye think ye have eternal life: and they are they which testify of Me."* ~ Not knowing God can be a hopeless feeling. If you're depressed, overwhelmed, discouraged, about to give up, or just don't have a reason to go on, don't give up. God has eternal joy and peace for you. Just open His Word and your heart (saved or not).

55. "Don't Look Now, but..." ~ Genesis 19:17: *"...Escape for thy life; look not behind thee, neither stay thou in all the plain; escape to the mountain, lest thou be consumed."* ~ The best is yet to come. You didn't come this far to stop or turn around, so head for the hills from which cometh your help.

56. "It's Not Your Fight" ~ 2 Chronicles 20:17: "*Ye shall not [need] to fight in this [battle]: set yourselves, stand ye [still], and see the salvation of the LORD...*" ~ Sometimes the hardest thing to do is nothing. God is our tag-team partner. Stop playing and tag Him in.

57. "In a Grave Situation?" ~ Ezekiel 37:13: "*And ye shall know that I [am] the LORD, when I have opened your graves, O my people, and brought you up out of your graves.*" ~ Maybe your grave was depression, financial debt, troubled relationships, sickness, and so on. God said it ain't over; you just need to move over and let Him handle it.

58. "Signed, Sealed, Delivered, I'm Yours" ~ Luke 23:46: *"And when Jesus had cried with a loud voice, He said, 'Father, into thy hands I commend my spirit:' and having said thus, He gave up the ghost."* ~ He (Jesus) held up His part of the deal. Now will you hold yours and receive what He (Jesus) delivered on the cross?

____

____

____

59. "Gotta Taste for Something Good?" ~ Psalm 34:8: *"O taste and see that the LORD [is] good: blessed [is] the man [that] trusteth in Him.* ~ No by-products, artificial coloring, sweetener, etc...pure wholesome GOOD!

____

____

____

60. "All Good Things Must Come to a Beginning" ~ Revelation 21:5: *"Behold, I make all things new. And He said unto me, Write: for these words are true* *and faithful.*" ~ So, what are you waiting on? Got bad news? Don't like the way things are currently going? Well, get a new beginning. Send all inquiries to God. He is our maker.

____

____

____

61. "Walk This Way" ~ 2 Corinthians 5:7: "*For we walk by faith, not by sight.*" ~ Don't limit yourself by what you see. Move past the barriers of your physical limitations and walk in faith. Peter walked on water; you can walk on the promises of God. So, stop looking and start walking.

____

____

____

62. "Delayed Don't Mean Denied" ~ Galatians 6:9: "*And let us not be weary in well doing: for in due season we shall reap, if we faint not.*" ~ This is to the singles, the unemployed, the sick, the heartbroken, the suicidal, the overlooked, and the burdened. Don't cash in your dreams because of the attacks of the devil.

63. "You're Greater Than That!" ~ 1 John 4:4: "*Ye are of God, little children, and have overcome them: because greater is He that is in you, than he that is in the world.*" ~ You can overcome anything with God. Just take a deep breath (of prayer) then exhale all (the doubts) of why you can't.

64. "The Handiwork of God" ~ Psalm 118:*24: "This [is] the day [which] the LORD hath made; we will rejoice and be glad in it.*" ~ Lord, thank you for another day. You didn't have to do it, but I'm so glad you did.

65. "Read Before Handling" ~ Joshua 6:18: "... *In any wise keep [yourselves] from the accursed thing, lest ye make [yourselves] accursed...*" ~ Some things shouldn't be handled due to cross contamination. It's not that you're too good for some people or things, but some people or things aren't good for you.

____

____

____

66. "This Day __/__/__" ~ Matthew 11:12: "...*The kingdom of heaven suffereth violence, and the violent take it by force.*" This is your canvas. What will you make of it?" You get one chance, so make God proud! Remember, He's entrusted us with it. Somebody didn't wake up this morning, so seize the day!

____

____

____

67. "It's All Good" ~ Romans 8:28: "*And we know that all things work together for good to them that love God, to them who are the called according to [His]* *purpose.*" ~ The good, the bad, and the ugly is all working in your favor. Remember God Is the master planner and nothing happens without his approval.

____

____

____

68. "What Did You Expect? ~ Jeremiah 29:11: "'*For I know the thoughts that I think toward you,' saith the LORD; 'thoughts of peace, and not of evil, to give you an expected end.'*" ~ It doesn't matter what they think or what your situation looks like, you must expect to triumph because it only matters what God thinks.
I expect a miracle today, if not sooner.

____

____

____

69. "Whatcha Looking at?" ~ 1 Samuel 16:7: "*But the LORD said unto Samuel, 'Look not on his countenance, or on the height of his stature; because I have refused him: for [the LORD seeth] not as man seeth; for man looketh on the outward appearance, but the LORD looketh on the* *heart.'"* ~ Be careful how you classify people because everybody ain't what you think you see.

____

____

____

70. "My Daddy Got It for Me" ~ Philippians 4:19: *"But my God shall supply all your need according to His riches in glory by Christ Jesus."* ~ If you're stressing over what you don't have, then start counting your blessings and by the time you're finished God will have given you just what you needed.

Correction.

____

____

____

71. "Gone with the Wind" ~ Luke 8:24: *"And they came to Him, and awoke Him, saying, 'Master, Master, we perish.' Then He arose, and rebuked the wind and the raging of the water: and they ceased, and there was a calm."* ~ Call on the Lord and see Him calm the storms in your life.

Poof... all your troubles are passed away.

____

____

____

72. "It's in the Works" ~ Romans 8:28: "*And we know that all things work together for good to them that love God, to them who are the called according to [His] purpose.*" ~ You must walk by faith and not by sight. Remind yourself, my eyes may see one thing, but my faith sees another.

Whose report will you believe?

____

____

____

73. "Who Is It....?" ~ Revelation 3:20: "*Behold, I stand at the door, and knock: if any man hear my voice, and open the door, I will come in to him, and will sup with him, and he with Me.* ~ ...Oh it's for you. Will you answer Him today? Sometimes we feel all alone, but God is steadily knocking.

____

____

____

74. "I Thought You Knew" ~ Isaiah 40:28: "*Hast thou not known? Hast thou not heard, [that] the everlasting God, the LORD, the Creator of the ends of the earth, fainteth not, neither is weary? [There is] no searching of his understanding.*" ~ Don't give up and don't forget God is still on the throne.
Delayed don't mean denied.

____

____

____

75. "I Thought You Knew" ~ 1 John 4:8: "*He that loveth not knoweth not God; for God is love.*" ~ Talk is cheap; actions speak. What have you done for someone other than me, myself and I lately? Well, let's do something about it TODAY, then give an update and share how it made a difference.
Somebody can use a blessing from you today!

76. "Rest in Peace" ~ Psalm 37:7: "*Rest in the LORD, and wait patiently for Him: fret not thyself because of him who prospereth in his way, because of the man who bringeth wicked devices to pass.*" ~ Stop trying to keep up with the Joneses; you don't know who they robbed, cheated, or stole from to get where you think you wanna be. What God has for you is for you, so be patient and watch God work.

77. "Come to Your Senses" ~ Luke 15:17: "*And when he came to himself, he said, 'How many hired servants of my father's have bread enough and to spare, and I perish with hunger!'*" ~ Your situation don't define you, but your response does. Don't forget who made you, and God don't make mistakes or failures. Say it loud, "I am Somebody!"

____

____

____

78. "Cut Me Some Slack" ~ 2 Peter 3:9: "*The Lord is not slack concerning His promise, as some men count slackness; but is longsuffering to usward, not willing that any should perish, but that all should come to repentance.*" ~ People may not give you a chance, but God has, so what will you do with it?

I'm just saying.

____

____

____

79. "The Possibilities Are Endless" ~ Matthew 19:26: "*But Jesus beheld [them], and said unto them, 'With men this is impossible; but with God all things are possible.*'" ~ Never put a question mark where God put a period. Take the hook out of your question mark and make it into an exclamation mark when speaking to your problem!

____

____

____

80. "What Is Today?" ~ Psalm 118:24: *"This [is] the day [which] the LORD hath made; we will rejoice and be glad in it."* ~ Yes, today is "Made It Day." As in God made it possible for us to _____, so in the midst of this day, remember to get your praise in.
Count your blessings today.
Well, how high did you count?

____

____

____

81. "Response Requested" ~ Proverbs 18:21: *"Death and life [are] in the power of the tongue: and they that love it shall eat the fruit thereof."* ~ In one of my prior motivation quotes I said, "Yes We Can!" I'm asking everyone to say what it is that you can do with the help of the Lord! Declare with your mouth!

____

____

____

82. "Yes We Can!" ~ Philippians 4:13: *"I can do all things through Christ which strengtheneth me."* ~ If God be for you, failure isn't an option, but a choice. Can your marriage work, can your kids go to college, can your body be healed, can your debt be erased? Yes, Yes, Yes and Yes. You can't do it, but God can!

____

____

____

83. "Excuse Me, I'm Working on It" ~ Psalm 139:23-24: *"Search me, O God, and know my heart: try me, and know my thoughts: And see if [there be any] wicked way in me, and lead me in the way everlasting."* ~ People say, "I ain't perfect" when they do something wrong but write off others when they make a mistake. Lord I need your help; I can't do it without you.
Excuse me while I work on me.

____

____

____

84. "To Thine Own Self Be True" ~ Philippians 4:8: *"Finally, brethren, whatsoever things are true, whatsoever things [are] honest, whatsoever things [are] just, whatsoever things [are] pure, whatsoever things [are] lovely, whatsoever things [are] of good report; if [there be] any virtue, and if [there be] any praise, think on these things."* ~ Life is too short to dwell on negatives of life. Trust God and live.

____

____

____

85. "Watch Your Step!" ~ Joshua 1:3: *"Every place that the sole of your foot shall tread upon, that have I given unto you..."* ~ Be careful where you tread. Don't go there; some things aren't worth the trip. Stay the course and walk the path God has laid before you.

____

____

____

86. "Is That Your Best Offer?" ~ Hebrews 13:15: "*By Him therefore let us offer the sacrifice of praise to God continually, that is, the fruit of [our] lips giving thanks to His name.*" ~ Is what you're offering an acceptable counteroffer to what God offers us through His Son Jesus? People, let's raise our praise. This ain't the game of football, but the game of life, and Jesus just made the winning play.

____

____

____

87. "Raise the Roof" ~ Mark 2:4: "*And when they could not come nigh unto Him for the press, they uncovered the roof where He was: and when they had broken [it] up, they let down the bed wherein the sick of the palsy lay.*" ~ Take the barriers off. Sometimes the circumstance calls for extra effort, so do what you have to do, but don't throw in the towel.

88. "You Have the Right to Remain Silent" ~ Exodus 14:14: "*The LORD shall fight for you, and ye shall hold your peace.* ~ You ain't gotta say a word, just watch God say it for you. He always has the last word.
Okay God, I'm on hush mode.

89. "What's Love Got to Do with It?" ~ John 3:16: "*For God so loved the world, that He gave his only begotten Son, that whosoever believeth in Him should not perish, but have everlasting life.*" ~ As far as I'm concerned (Tina), it's got everything to do with it.
If you got it flaunt it.

90. "The Price Is Right" ~ 1 Corinthians 6:20: "*For ye are bought with a price: therefore glorify God in your body, and in your spirit, which are God's.*" ~ Jesus paid it all, all to Him I owe. Car = $20,000, Home = $300,000, Redemption = Priceless. Are you making payments on your IOU?

____

____

____

91. "Well It's That Time" ~ Ecclesiastes 3:2: "*A time to be born, and a time to die; a time to plant, and a time to pluck up [that which is] planted ...*" ~ Thanks for all the birthday acknowledgements on August 20th. I'm plucking up every post and planting a thank you. I love each and every one of you! Thank You!

____

____

____

92. "You Ain't Seen Nothing Yet" ~ 1 Corinthians 2:9: "*But as it is written, Eye hath not seen, nor ear heard,* *neither have entered into the heart of man, the things which God hath prepared for them that love Him."* ~ Keep trusting and believing in God's Word and He will work it out. Remember, delayed don't mean denied. It shall come to pass.

____

____

____

93. "I-O-U" ~ Romans 13:8: *"Owe no man anything, but to love one another: for he that loveth another hath fulfilled the law."* ~ We owe it to one another to love. Dear God, thank you for loving me to life. You loved us when we didn't love ourselves and when others gave up on us you didn't. Have you paid on your installment today?

____

____

____

94. "Possession Is 9/10 of the Law" ~ Genesis 2:23: *"And Adam said, 'This [is] now bone of my bones, and flesh of my flesh: she shall be called Woman, because she was taken out of Man.'"* ~ Men don't leave your woman unprotected. Take pride in what God gave you. After all she's bone of your bone and flesh of your flesh. If your teeth bite your tongue will you pull out your teeth or be more careful next time?

____

____

____

95. "Favor Ain't Fair" ~ Matthew 5:45: "... *For He maketh His sun to rise on the evil and on the good, and sendeth rain on the just and on the unjust.* ~ What this means is you got the job, you're healed, you're getting the promotion, an unexpected blessing is about to overtake you because God simply favors you over somebody else's qualifications. Need proof you got the job, and you weren't the most qualified? Some of you got the girl/guy and wasn't the 1st choice; the doctor said there's no cure for your illness, but 7 years later you're still here. FAVOR AIN'T FAIR!!!

____

____

____

96. "Some Things Are Better Left Unsaid" ~ Exodus 14:14: "*The LORD shall fight for you, and ye shall hold your peace.*" ~ Hold your peace and let the Lord fight your battle. Victory, victory shall be mine.

____

____

____

97. "What Goes up Must Come down" ~ Matthew 18:18: "*Verily I say unto you, Whatsoever ye shall bind on earth shall be bound in heaven: and whatsoever ye shall loose on earth shall be loosed in heaven.*" ~ Your miracle, your break-through, your answer starts with you and ends with God, so send that request to God and see if He won't answer.

It's a closed mouth that don't get fed.

____

____

____

98. "Don't Call Me; I'll Call You" ~ Acts 2:21: "*And it shall come to pass, [that] whosoever shall call on the* *name of the Lord shall be saved.*" ~ Don't wait for God to call you home; you'd better learn to call Him NOW!

99. "Lord, Jesus I Need to Get Laid! ~ Luke 4:40: "*Now when the sun was setting, all they that had any sick with divers diseases brought them unto Him; and He LAID His hands on every one of them, and healed them.*" ~ Just one touch by the King will rock your world. Tom, Dick, and Harry can't do you like Jesus, so what are you waiting on? He's waiting to lay it on! He had to get your attention somehow!□□

100a. "I Need a 40!" ~ Psalm 40:1: "*I waited patiently for the LORD; and He inclined unto me, and heard my cry.*" ~ Turn to God and not the bottle. He'll hear your cry; the bottle will make you cry. Yes, God serves 40's.

100b. "Who Could Use a 40 Right Now?" ~ Isaiah 40:29: "*He giveth power to the faint; and to [them that have] no might He increaseth strength.*" ~ I know it's early, but this 40 doesn't leave you with bad side effects. We all can use a little pick-me-up after a long week.

101. "Wait for It...Wait for It..." ~ Psalm 37:7: "*Rest in the LORD, and wait patiently for Him: fret not thyself because of him who prospereth in his way, because of the man who bringeth wicked devices to pass.*" ~Remember if you want it bad enough, then wait. The most valued things in life are worth the wait.

102. "Just Hold on" ~ *Psalms 27:14 - Wait on the Lord: be of good courage, and he shall strengthen thine heart: wait I say, on the Lord."* ~ The air quality is best after a downpour of rain. If you're going through something, find a stable covering, hold on, and wait out the storm, because your better days come after you weather the storms of life.

____

____

____

103. Here's a Good "401K Plan" ~ Psalm 40:1: "*I waited patiently for the LORD; and He inclined unto me, and heard my cry.*" ~ With this plan you'll need to invest some fasting and praying. Then, with patience, watch God turn your investment around and double it. Anyone know what I'm talking about, say Amen!

____

____

____

104. [Judge opens envelope] - "You Are Not the Father!" ~ Psalm 27:10: "*When my father and my mother forsake me, then the LORD will take me up.*" ~ You may not know or have a relationship with one or both parents, but God has a way of filling in, so don't feel that you're forsaken. God will take up the slack!

___

___

___

105. "I Yam What I Yam" ~ 1 Peter 2:9: "*But ye [are] a chosen generation, a royal priesthood, an holy nation, a peculiar people; that ye should shew forth the praises of Him who hath called you out of darkness into His marvelous light.*" ~ When Bluto (the devil) is beating you down, reach for your spinach (praise/worship). It works every time.

___

___

___

106. "Deuces" ~ John 19:30: "*When Jesus therefore had received the vinegar, He said, 'It is finished:' and He bowed His head, and gave up the ghost.* ~ Whatever you're going through, it's over when God says it's over. Deuces = When you flip the middle finger and index finger together. Giving the "peace out" when you're done with a person...physically, mentally, or spiritually.

____

____

____

107. "It Ain't What It Looks Like" ~ Mark 8:24: *And he looked up, and said, I see men as trees, walking.* ~ God ain't finished performing your miracle, so rub your eyes, give it a minute, and take another look.

____

____

____

108. "Black and Beautiful" ~ Song of Solomon 1:5: "*I [am] black, but comely....*" ~ Comely is defined as pleasant to look at; attractive. Let's celebrate Black History Month every month, by showing everyone what it means to be "B&B." Take pride in your God, family, community, and self. Remember I am who God made me to be and that's B&B.

____

____

____

109. "That's What You Get! ~ Matthew 7:7: "*Ask, and it shall be given you; seek, and ye shall find; knock, and it shall be opened unto you...*" ~ When you take your petitions to the Lord, He can and will respond.

____

____

____

110. "Purple Reign" ~ John 19:5: "*Then came Jesus forth, wearing the crown of thorns, and the purple robe. And Pilate saith unto them, Behold the man!*" ~ He went to the cross for you and me. Accept the Man and you can laugh when it rains (like Prince laughing in the purple rain)!

____

____

____

111. "Stirred Not Shaken" ~ 2 Thessalonians 2:2: *"That ye be not soon shaken in mind, or be troubled, neither by spirit, nor by word, nor by letter as from us, as that the day of Christ is at hand."* ~ Acting now on God's word means you can be at peace, but to ignore means an uneasy lifestyle.

____

____

____

112. "Don't Sweat the Small Stuff" ~ Luke 22:24: *"And being in an agony He (Jesus) prayed more earnestly: and his sweat was as it were great drops of blood falling down to the ground."* ~ Jesus already sweated over something far greater than your glands could ever produce and that was going to the cross for the salvation of our souls.

____

____

____

113. "Because I Said So!" ~ Mark 11:23: "*For verily I say unto you, that whosoever shall say unto this mountain, 'Be thou removed, and be thou cast into the sea;' and shall not doubt in his heart but shall believe that those things which he saith shall come to pass; he shall have whatsoever he saith.*" ~ Speak over your problem: Problem, you are the weakest link; goodbye!

____

____

____

114. "I Told You SO!" ~ John 3:16: "*For God SO loved the world, that He gave his only begotten Son, that whosoever believeth in Him should not perish, but have everlasting life.*" ~ No matter what failures people have held over you or even worse you have held over yourself, remember God said, "SO," I still loved you enough to nail it to the cross, SO, leave the pity party and CROSS over to the redeemed and highly favored status. (Deuces).

____

____

____

115. [In my Urkel voice] "Did I Do That?" ~ Philippians 4:13: *"I can do all things through Christ which strengtheneth me."* ~ Don't count yourself out; with God anything is possible.

A little railroad engine was waiting for the next call when a long train of freight-cars asked a large engine in the roundhouse to take it over the hill. "I can't; that is too much of a pull for me," said the great engine built for hard work. Then the train asked another engine, and another, only to hear excuses and be refused. In desperation, the train asked the little switch engine to draw it up the grade and down on the other side. "I think I can," puffed the little locomotive, and put itself in front of the great heavy train. As it went on the little engine kept bravely puffing faster and faster, "I think I can, I think I can, I think I can." As it neared the top of the grade, which had so discouraged the larger engines, it went more slowly. However, it still kept saying, "I—think—I—can, I—think—I—can." It reached the top by drawing on bravery and then went on down the grade, congratulating itself by saying, "I thought I could, I thought I could." (Written by Watty Piper)

____

____

____

116. "Love Connection" ~ John 15:4: "*Abide in me, and I in you. As the branch cannot bear fruit of itself, except it abide in the vine; no more can ye, except ye abide in me.*" ~ Let nothing or anyone separate you from the love of God. We can't do it without Him.

____

____

____

Dear Valley Reader,

If you're going through a valley, remember that a journey has two points: a beginning and an ending. Don't get stuck in the valley and don't turn around. If God brought you to it, He will bring you through it.

The only way to get to your mountain-top experience is to go through your valley low. If you can't run, jog, if you can't jog, walk, if you can't walk, crawl, if you can't crawl call an Uber, but by any means necessary, don't set up camp in the valley. It is not your home and was never meant to be.

Don't let people or situations define your residence. Heaven is your goal, not a valley full of dry bones. While fretting over your valley, remember that God is leading you and goodness and mercy are following you. Therefore, you're surrounded.

The next time you want to ask the Lord, why the valley, think about this book, think about what's on the other end of the valley, think about who's in control of your destiny, think about if you don't go, think about God's promise; then pick yourself up and go...In the words of Jenny (in the movie - Forrest Gump), "Run, Forrest, Run."

God bless you,
George E. Robinson, Author

ADDITIONAL NOTE SPACE

AUTHOR'S BIOGRAPHICAL SKETCH

George E. Robinson is a first-time author who grew up in Los Angeles, CA and currently resides in the Riverside area. George has dedicated a great portion of his life to ministry. He served as the founding Pastor of True Origin for 6 years prior to returning to Greater Deliverance Church, where he has held such positions as Youth Pastor, Prayer Intercessor, Sunday School Superintendent, Board Member, and right-hand man to Pastor Mark Leonard.

George is married to Carla, whom he fondly refers to as "Butterscotch." He is a proud father to Danielle, George, Evan, and Marcus.

George's motto when it comes to ministry is to make it "Real, Practical, and Relevant (RPR)." He constantly instills this motto every Sunday during Sunday School with staff and students.

George is currently looking to expand the ministry with the launch of RPR Ministries, which will address everyday issues that affect people. The focus is addressing life issues from a real, practical, and relevant way.

George was ordained in the Church of God in Christ, Inc. He graduated from Washington Preparatory High School with honors and is positioned to complete his B.A. in Business Administration, from the University of Redlands. During down times, George enjoys playing golf (been a while), and spending time with family.

If there is one thing he can leave with you, it is this: We all go through various seasons in life and some are difficult, but remember, your winter must come, so your spring can bring forth your promise!

AUTHOR'S CONTACT INFORMATION

Email:

lordwhythevalley@gmail.com

Facebook:

https://www.facebook.com/george.e.robinson

Twitter:

gerlife67

Instagram:
67tolife

LinkedIn:
gerlife67 (www.linkedin.com/in/gerlife67)

www.ingramcontent.com/pod-product-compliance
Lightning Source LLC
LaVergne TN
LVHW091313080426
835510LV00007B/479
9781735821153